Sou

CAROLE HANDSLIP

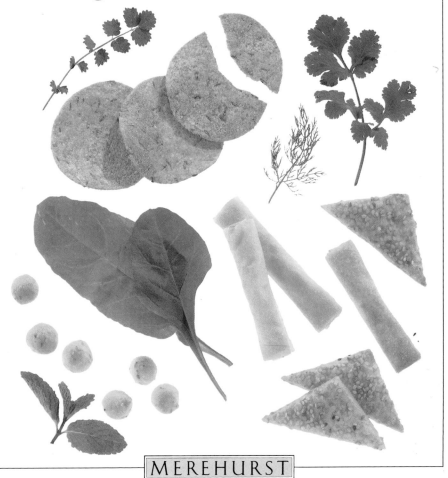

MEREHURST

LONDON

Contents

Managing Editor: Janet Illsley
Photographer: Ken Field
Designer: Sue Storey
Food Stylist: Carole Handslip
Photographic Stylist: Maria Jacques
Typeset by Angel Graphics
Colour separation by Fotographics, UK - Hong Kong
Printed in Italy by New Interlitho S.p.A.

Published 1991 by Merehurst Ltd,
Ferry House, 51/57 Lacy Road, Putney, London SW15 1PR

© Merehurst Ltd

ISBN: 1 85391 183 6 (Cased)
ISBN: 1 85391 260 3 (Paperback)

NOTES
All spoon measures are level: 1 tablespoon = 15ml spoon;
1 teaspoon = 5ml spoon.
Use fresh herbs and freshly ground black pepper unless otherwise stated.

Introduction

Soups are highly versatile, ranging from delicately flavoured creamy concoctions to hearty farmhouse *potages*. Indeed, many are sustaining enough to provide a meal in themselves. Such is the variety of soups you can prepare, it is always possible to choose one to serve as a starter. They can be informal or formal, warm and comforting or cool and refreshing, suitable for dinner party and bonfire alike.

Stock is all-important when making a soup and, although the cubed variety will suffice if time is short, the result will be far superior if you make your own stock. I often prepare a large quantity and freeze it in convenient amounts for future use. It's well worth reducing the stock by boiling to give a greater concentration of flavour and to take up less space in the freezer.

Many soups can be served just as they are, simply with fresh crusty bread, but some really benefit from a little added interest. Throughout the book you will find accompaniment ideas, which are largely interchangeable. Croûtons, crisply fried bacon, grated gruyère and Parmesan all add flavour and texture. Those which take longer to make – such as sablés and crackers – can be prepared ahead. Try serving flavoured breads – olive bread goes well with many soups. Garlic bread makes a good accompaniment to the more substantial soups and, surprisingly, children often love it.

Soups are, above all, most rewarding to make – quick and easy – yet tasty to savour. I hope your greatest difficulty will be simply which soup to try first from this collection!

Carole Handslip.

Roquefort & Almond Soup

Roquefort and almonds marry perfectly in this creamy, smooth-textured soup. However, you could substitute Stilton if you prefer. Cheese profiteroles (below) make an ideal crisp accompaniment.

1 tablespoon sunflower oil
1 clove garlic, crushed
1 tablespoon flour
625ml (1 pint/2½ cups) milk
60g (2oz/½ cup) ground
  almonds
90g (3 oz) Roquefort cheese

2 tablespoons chopped chervil
  or parsley
salt and pepper to taste
TO SERVE:
chervil or parsley sprigs
cheese profiteroles (see below)

1 Heat the oil in a pan, add the garlic and fry gently for 1 minute. Remove from the heat and stir in the flour. Stir in 155ml (5 fl oz/⅔ cup) of the milk. Add the ground almonds and stir until blended. Add the remaining milk, return to the heat and bring to the boil. Cook, stirring, for 3 minutes until thickened.

2 Crumble in the Roquefort, add the herbs and stir over a gentle heat until the cheese has melted. Add seasoning.

3 Serve garnished with chervil or parsley and accompanied by cheese profiteroles. *Serves 6.*

CHEESE PROFITEROLES: Sift 5 tablespoons flour with ½ teaspoon mustard and a pinch each of cayenne pepper and salt. Melt 30g (1oz) butter or margarine in a pan, add 75ml (2½ fl oz/⅓ cup) water and bring to the boil. Add the flour mixture all at once, remove from the heat and beat vigorously until the mixture leaves the sides of the pan clean. Gradually add 1 beaten egg, beating vigorously. Beat in 30g (1oz/¼ cup) finely grated Cheddar cheese, 2 table-spoons Parmesan, and 1 tablespoon toasted sesame seeds.

Turn into a piping bag fitted with a 5mm (¼ inch) plain nozzle and pipe blobs, each the size of a large pea, on to a non-stick baking sheet. Bake in a preheated oven at 190C (375F/Gas 5) for 15-17 minutes until golden.

Mushroom & Madeira Soup

375g (12oz) field mushrooms
45g (1½oz) butter
2 cloves garlic, chopped
2 tablespoons chopped parsley
1 bay leaf
1 thyme sprig

60ml (2 fl oz / ¼ cup) Madeira
2 tablespoons flour
785ml (1¼ pints / 3 cups)
  chicken stock
155ml (5 fl oz / ⅔ cup) double
  (thick) cream

1 Chop mushrooms very finely. Melt butter in a saucepan, add mushrooms and garlic and fry gently for 10 minutes. Add the herbs and Madeira and cook for 2-3 minutes.
2 Stir in the flour, gradually add the stock and bring to the boil, stirring. Cook for 5 minutes, then remove the bay leaf and thyme. Stir in the cream to serve. *Serves 4-6.*

Carrot & Coriander Soup

1 tablespoon oil
1 onion, chopped
2 teaspoons ground coriander
1 clove garlic, chopped
500g (1lb) carrots, chopped
940ml (1½ pints / 3¾ cups)
  chicken stock

15g (½oz) butter
1 tablespoon flour
155ml (5 fl oz / ⅔ cup) single
  (light) cream
salt and pepper to taste
coriander sprigs to garnish

1 Heat the oil in a pan and fry the onion until softened. Add the coriander, garlic and carrots and fry for 1 minute.
2 Pour in the stock, bring to the boil, cover and cook for 30 minutes until the carrots are tender. Cool slightly, then pour into a blender or food processor and work to a purée.
3 Melt the butter in the cleaned pan, stir in the flour, then pour in the blended soup and cook for 2 minutes until thickened. Stir in the cream and seasoning.
4 Serve garnished with coriander. *Serves 4-6.*

Spinach & Gruyère Soup

This tasty soup is delicious served with filo cigarettes (below). Instead of fresh spinach, defrosted frozen spinach can be used.

2 tablespoons oil
1 onion, chopped
2 sticks celery, chopped
1 tablespoon flour
470ml (3/4 pint/1 1/4 cups)
* vegetable stock or water*
500g (1lb) spinach
1/4 teaspoon grated nutmeg

bouquet garni
salt and pepper to taste
470ml (3/4 pint/1 1/4 cups) milk
2 egg yolks
juice of 1/2 lemon
60g (2oz) Gruyère cheese,
* grated*

1 Heat the oil in a saucepan, add the onion and celery and fry until softened. Remove from the heat and stir in the flour, then gradually add the stock or water, stirring until evenly blended. Bring to the boil, stirring.

2 Add the spinach, pressing it down until it has wilted. Add the nutmeg, bouquet garni and seasoning. Cover and cook gently for 20 minutes. Discard the bouquet garni.

3 Cool slightly, then pour the soup into a food processor or blender and work to a smooth purée. Return to the rinsed-out pan, add the milk and reheat.

4 In a bowl, mix together the egg yolks and lemon juice, then add a ladleful of soup and stir well. Pour back into the soup and cook gently, stirring, until thickened; do not boil.

5 Spoon into individual bowls and sprinkle with the Gruyère. Serve with filo cigarettes, if desired. *Serves 6.*

FILO CIGARETTES: Mix 90g (3oz) ricotta or feta cheese with 1 tablespoon chopped dill or parsley, adding a little milk to moisten if necessary. Take 4 sheets of filo pastry and cut each into 5 strips, measuring 7.5 x 25cm (3 x 10 inches); keep covered. Brush each strip with melted butter, put a little filling at one end and roll up, folding in the ends. Put on a baking sheet, brush with butter and bake in a preheated oven at 190C (375F/Gas 5) for 10-12 minutes until golden.

VEGETABLE & NUT SOUPS

Cauliflower & Cress Soup

A delicate smooth soup, especially good served with a cheesy accompaniment, such as cheese sablés (below).

1 bunch watercress	*785ml (1¼ pints/3 cups)*
2 tablespoons oil	*chicken stock*
1 onion, chopped	*salt and pepper to taste*
1 small cauliflower, chopped	*4 tablespoons single (light)*
	cream

1 Roughly chop the watercress. Heat the oil in a pan, add the onion and watercress, cover and cook gently for about 10 minutes until softened.

2 Add the cauliflower, stock and seasoning. Bring to the boil, cover and simmer gently for 20 minutes until the cauliflower is cooked.

3 Cool slightly, then pour into a blender or food processor and blend until smooth. Return to the pan and heat through. Pour into individual serving bowls and swirl in the cream. Serve with cheese sablés or crusty bread *Serves 6.*

CHEESE SABLÉS: Sift 90g (3oz/¾ cup) plain flour, 1 teaspoon mustard and a pinch each of cayenne and salt together into a bowl. Rub in 60g (2oz) butter. Add 60g (2oz) grated strong Cheddar cheese and 1 egg yolk; mix to a firm dough. Knead lightly, then roll out thinly on a floured surface to a rectangle, 28 x 15cm (11 x 6 inches). Cut into three 5cm (2 inch) wide strips, brush with egg white and sprinkle with toasted sesame seeds. Cut into 36 small triangles. Chill for 15 minutes. Bake in a preheated oven 190C (375F/Gas 5) for 15 minutes until golden.

Jerusalem Artichoke Soup

2 tablespoons oil
1 large onion, chopped
500g (1lb) Jerusalem
   artichokes, scrubbed and
   roughly chopped
785ml (1¼ pints/3 cups)
   chicken stock

salt and pepper to taste
155ml (5 fl oz/⅔ cup) single
   (light) cream
1 teaspoon lemon juice
herb sprigs to garnish

1 Heat the oil in a pan, add the onion and cook until softened. Add the artichokes and cook gently, stirring occasionally, for 10 minutes. Add the stock and seasoning. Bring to the boil, cover and simmer gently for about 45 minutes.
2 Cool slightly, then work in a blender or food processor until smooth. Sieve to obtain a really smooth texture. Return to the pan, add the cream and lemon juice and reheat. Serve garnished with herbs. *Serves 4.*

Red Pepper Soup

4 red peppers, halved, cored
   and seeded
1 tablespoon oil
1 onion, chopped
1 clove garlic, chopped
2 teaspoons paprika

4 tomatoes, skinned and seeded
625ml (1 pint/2½ cups)
   vegetable stock or water
salt to taste
4 tablespoons thick sour cream
chives to garnish

1 Lay the pepper halves, rounded side up, on a grill pan and grill for 8-10 minutes until charred. Peel off the skins under cold running water and chop the flesh roughly.
2 Heat the oil in a pan, add the onion and garlic and fry gently until softened. Add the paprika and cook gently for 30 seconds. Stir in the tomatoes and stock. Transfer to a blender or food processor, add the red peppers and blend until smooth.
3 Season, heat through, then pour into individual bowls. Swirl in the sour cream and garnish with chives. *Serves 4.*

Cucumber & Dill Soup

Cooked cucumber has a subtle interesting flavour and tastes quite different from its raw counterpart. This delicate soup is delicious served hot or cold. Potato croûtons (below) make a good accompaniment.

2 tablespoons oil
1 onion, chopped
2 cucumbers, peeled and
   roughly chopped
250g (8oz) potato, roughly
   chopped

785ml (1¼ pints/3 cups)
   chicken stock
1 bay leaf
salt and pepper to taste
155ml (5 fl oz/⅔ cup) thick sour
   cream
1 tablespoon chopped dill

1 Heat the oil in a pan, add the onion and fry until softened. Add the cucumber and potato and cook for 5 minutes, stirring occasionally.

2 Add the stock, bay leaf and seasoning. Bring to the boil, cover and cook gently for 20 minutes.

3 Remove the bay leaf, pour the soup into a blender or food processor and blend until smooth. Add the sour cream and blend again.

4 Return the soup to the pan, stir in the chopped dill and reheat gently, but do not boil.

5 Pour into individual soup bowls and serve with potato croutons, if wished. *Serves 4-6.*

POTATO CROÛTONS: Parboil 2 potatoes in boiling water for 4 minutes, then drain and cut into small dice while still warm. Pour oil into a small pan to a depth of 1cm (½ inch) and place over moderate heat. When hot, add the potato and fry, stirring, for a few seconds until evenly browned. Drain on absorbent kitchen paper and sprinkle lightly with salt.

Pumpkin Soup

1 tablespoon oil
1 onion, chopped
1 clove garlic, chopped
750g (1 1/2 lb) pumpkin, peeled
  and roughly chopped
2 potatoes, roughly chopped
3 large tomatoes, peeled and
  chopped

940ml (1 1/2 pints/3 3/4 cups)
  vegetable stock or water
bouquet garni
salt and pepper to taste
4 tablespoons double (thick)
  cream
TO SERVE:
croûtons (page 60)

1 Heat the oil in a pan and fry the onion and garlic until softened. Add the pumpkin, potatoes, tomatoes, stock or water, bouquet garni and seasoning. Bring to the boil, cover and simmer gently for 25 minutes until pumpkin is tender.
2 Cool slightly, discard bouquet garni, then purée soup in a blender or food processor until smooth. Reheat in the pan, stir in the cream and serve with croûtons. *Serves 6.*

Chestnut & Cranberry Soup

1 tablespoon oil
1 onion, chopped
2 sticks celery, chopped
940ml (1 1/2 pints/3 3/4 cups)
  vegetable stock
bouquet garni
salt and pepper to taste

500g (1lb) peeled cooked
  chestnuts, or can unsweetened
  chestnut purée
60g (2oz) cranberries
60ml (2 fl oz/1/4 cups) port
parsley sprigs to garnish

1 Heat the oil in a pan and fry the onion until softened. Add the celery, stock, bouquet garni and seasoning. Bring to the boil, cover and simmer gently for 15 minutes.
2 Add the chestnuts and cranberries, and simmer for 15 minutes. Discard the bouquet garni and set aside a few cranberries for garnish. Allow the soup to cool slightly, then purée in a blender or food processor until smooth.
3 Return to the pan, add the port, check the seasoning and serve garnished with the cranberries and parsley. *Serves 6.*

Cock-a-Leekie

A wonderful soup from Scotland, which sometimes has a few prunes added. Traditionally a capon or boiling fowl is used, as the long slow cooking ensures its tenderness. You can of course use chicken instead.

1 capon, boiling fowl or chicken	*1.75 litres (3 pints/7½ cups)*
1 onion, quartered	*water*
2 carrots, roughly chopped	*45g (1½oz) butter*
bouquet garni	*750g (1½lb) leeks, sliced into*
6 peppercorns	*rings*
1 teaspoon salt	*2 tablespoons chopped parsley*

1 Put the bird and its giblets into a large saucepan with the onion, carrots, bouquet garni, peppercorns and salt, then add the water. Bring to the boil and skim off any scum that rises to the surface. Cover and simmer gently for 1¼-1½ hours until the poultry is cooked; a boiling fowl will take a little longer.

2 Lift out the poultry. Strain the stock, allow to cool, then refrigerate until the fat becomes solid. Discard the fat.

3 Remove the breast from the bird and reserve for another dish. Remove the skin from the wings and legs and cut the meat into fairly large pieces.

4 Heat the butter in a pan, add the leeks, cover and cook very gently for 10 minutes until softened. Add the stock and seasoning. Bring to the boil, cover and simmer gently for 15 minutes. Add the chicken and parsley, reheat for a few minutes and serve. *Serves 6-8.*

Black Bean & Coriander Soup

2 tablespoons oil
1 onion, chopped
2 sticks celery, chopped
2 cloves garlic, chopped
1 teaspoon chilli powder
1 teaspoon ground cumin
397g (14oz) can chopped
    tomatoes

1.25 litres (2 pints/5 cups)
    vegetable stock or water
250g (8oz) black beans, soaked
    overnight and drained
1 tablespoon tomato purée
    (paste)
2 tablespoons chopped coriander
salt and pepper to taste

1 Heat the oil in a saucepan and fry the onion and celery until softened. Add the garlic and spices and fry gently for 1 minute.

2 Add the tomatoes, stock or water, black beans and tomato purée (paste). Bring to the boil and boil steadily for 10 minutes. Cover and simmer gently for about 1¾ hours until the beans are tender.

3 Add the coriander and seasoning. Serve with crusty bread. *Serves 6-8.*

Sweetcorn Chowder

1 tablespoon oil
1 large onion, chopped
500g (1lb) potatoes, chopped
625ml (1 pint/2½ cups) milk
1 bay leaf
salt and pepper to taste

500g (1lb) frozen sweetcorn
90g (3oz) streaky bacon, rind
    removed, chopped
2 tablespoons chopped parsley
125g (4oz) peeled prawns

1 Heat the oil in a saucepan, add the onion gnd fry until softened. Add the potatoes, milk, bay leaf and seasoning. Bring to the boil, cover and cook for 10 minutes. Add the sweetcorn and cook for a further 10-15 minutes until the sweetcorn and potatoes are tender. Discard the bay leaf.

2 Fry the bacon in its own fat until crisp; add to the soup with the parsley and prawns and heat through. *Serves 4.*

Scotch Broth

A comforting, homely soup, and a very nourishing one, too. As long as you include the basics of lamb and barley, you can use any vegetables you have to hand. Use scrag end or middle neck of lamb for this broth.

1kg (2lb) neck of lamb, excess fat removed
2.25 litres (4 pints/10 cups) water
60g (2oz/¼ cup) pot barley
bouquet garni
2 onions, chopped

2 sticks celery, chopped
2 carrots, chopped
1 leek, sliced
1 swede, chopped
salt and pepper to taste
2 tablespoons chopped parsley

1 Put the lamb in a large pan with the water, barley and bouquet garni. Bring slowly to the boil and remove any scum that rises to the surface, using a slotted spoon. Cover and simmer gently for 2 hours.

2 Add the vegetables and cook for a further 40 minutes. Discard the bouquet garni.

3 Lift the pieces of meat out the soup and leave until cool enough to handle. Remove the lamb from the bone, discard the fat and chop the meat into small pieces.

4 Using a tablespoon, remove as much fat from the surface of the soup as possible; then run absorbent kitchen paper across the surface to remove the rest.

5 Return the meat to the pan with the parsley, check the seasoning and heat through. *Serves 4-6.*

NOTE: If you have time, prepare the soup ahead and allow to cool at the end of step 3, then chill in the refrigerator until the fat becomes solid. Remove the fat layer. Reheat the soup as required.

Thai Tom Yum Soup

This typically Thai soup is a blend of lemon grass, lime and fish sauce. It may contain pieces of shellfish, pork, beef or chicken. Oriental fish sauce – or *nam pla* – imparts a characteristic flavour. It is made by layering fresh anchovies and salt in wooden barrels and leaving them to ferment. Fish sauce and lime leaves are obtainable from oriental stores.

1.25 litres (2 pints/5 cups) fish stock
3 lime leaves (fresh or frozen)
1 stalk lemon grass, crushed
1-2 chillies
250g (8oz) squid, cleaned and cut into rings

2 cloves garlic, chopped
2 tablespoons fish sauce
185g (6oz) peeled prawns
juice of 1 lime
salt to taste
1 tablespoon chopped coriander leaves

1 Put the fish stock, lime leaves and lemon grass in a pan and bring to the boil. Cover and simmer gently for 5 minutes.
2 Cut the chillies into rings, discarding the seeds unless you want a fiery hot soup! Add the chilli rings to the pan with the squid, garlic and fish sauce and cook for a further 10 minutes.
3 Add the prawns and heat through, then stir in the lime juice and salt.
4 Pour into individual bowls and sprinkle with the coriander.
Serves 4.

Prawn & Mushroom Soup

60g (2oz) dried rice stick
   noodles, broken into pieces
1½ tablespoons groundnut oil
125g (4oz) shitake or chestnut
   mushrooms, sliced
1 clove garlic, finely chopped
1½ teaspoons light soy sauce

940ml (1½ pints/3 cups)
   chicken stock
1 teaspoon sesame oil
salt and pepper to taste
90g (3oz) peeled prawns
1 bunch watercress, chopped

1 Soak the noodles in warm water for 10 minutes until softened, then drain thoroughly.

2 Heat the oil in a pan, add the mushrooms and garlic and fry briskly for 2 minutes, stirring occasionally.

3 Add the soy sauce, stock, sesame oil and seasoning. Bring to the boil and simmer gently for 2 minutes. Add the prawns and watercress and heat through. *Serves 4-6.*

Egg Flower Soup

This is one of the simplest and most basic of Chinese soups. Add the egg carefully – simply trickle it into the hot stock gradually from a fork, or chopsticks, and it will set in strands which look like flowers.

8 spring onions (green shallots),
   thinly sliced
1 teaspoon sesame oil
940ml (1½ pints/3 cups) chicken
   stock

1 tablespoon light soy sauce
salt and pepper to taste
1 egg, lightly whisked

1 Divide the spring onions (shallots) between 4 individual bowls and sprinkle with a few drops of sesame oil.

2 Put the stock into a saucepan and bring to the boil. Add the soy sauce and seasoning. Turn off the heat, then trickle in the egg in a thin stream, trailing it over the surface in a figure-of-eight movement; do not stir.

3 As soon as the egg sets – within about 30 seconds – ladle the soup into the bowls and serve. *Serves 4.*

Wonton Soup

Wontons are small savoury dumplings, traditionally served in a well-flavoured broth. Wonton wrappers are made from the same wheat dough as egg noodles, cut in 7.5cm (3 inch) squares. They are sold in packets – either fresh or frozen – in Chinese supermarkets.

16 wonton wrappers
WONTON FILLING:
125g (4oz) minced pork
2 teaspoons soy sauce
2 teaspoons sherry
½ teaspoon cornflour
1 teaspoon sesame oil
salt and pepper

SOUP:
940ml (1½ pints/3 cups)
  chicken stock
1 tablespoon soy sauce
2 tablespoons sherry
1 teaspoon sesame oil
4 spring onions (green shallots),
  sliced
125g (4oz) Pak choi, shredded
90g (3oz) shitake or chestnut
  mushrooms, sliced

1 In a bowl, mix together all the ingredients for the wonton filling until well blended. Lay the wonton wrappers on a work surface and place a teaspoonful of filling on each one. Dampen the edges, bring up the sides of each wrapper and pinch together at the top to seal.

2 Bring a large pan of salted water to the boil, add the wontons and cook for 4 minutes. Remove with a slotted spoon and keep warm.

3 Put the chicken stock in a large saucepan and bring to the boil. Add the soy sauce, sherry, seasoning, sesame oil, spring onions (shallots), pak choi and mushrooms and simmer for 2 minutes.

4 Divide the wontons between the soup bowls and spoon the soup over them. *Serves 4.*

PAK CHOI & TOFU SOUP: Omit the wontons. Start at stage 3, adding 315g (10oz) bean curd in 1cm (½ inch) cubes instead of the mushrooms and cook for an extra 2-3 minutes.

Prawn & Sweetcorn Soup

A popular Cantonese soup which can be made with prawns or
white crab meat if you prefer.

785ml (1¼ pints/3 cups)
chicken stock
1 teaspoon finely chopped root
(green) ginger
315g (10oz) frozen sweetcorn
salt and pepper to taste
1 tablespoon cornflour

1 tablespoon dry sherry
125g (4oz) peeled prawns
3 spring onions (green shallots),
thinly sliced diagonally
1 egg
1 tablespoon sesame oil

1 Put the stock into a large saucepan with the ginger,
sweetcorn and seasoning. Bring to the boil, cover and
simmer for 10 minutes.
2 Blend the cornflour with the sherry, then add to the soup
with the prawns and spring onions (shallots). Cook, stirring,
until thickened.
3 In a bowl, whisk the egg and sesame oil together with a
fork until well blended. Turn off the heat, then trickle the
egg in a thin stream over the soup from the fork, trailing it
over the surface in a figure-of-eight movement; do not stir.
4 As soon as the egg sets – within about 30 seconds – ladle
the soup into bowls. Serve immediately. *Serves 4.*

Hot & Sour Soup

This Northern Chinese peasant soup is sharp and spicy with a glutinous consistency. Bean thread noodles – also known as cellophane or transparent noodles – are made from ground mung beans. They are sold in small bundles in oriental stores.

125g (4oz) lean pork, cut into thin strips
30g (1oz) dried mushrooms
30g (1oz) bean thread noodles
3 tablespoons rice vinegar
1 teaspoon sesame oil
2 tablespoons dark soy sauce
2 teaspoons sugar
1 teaspoon chilli sauce
1½ tablespoons cornflour

625ml (1 pint/2½ cups) strong chicken stock
315g (10oz) bean curd, drained and cut into 1cm (½ inch) cubes
1 egg, lightly whisked
4 spring onions (green shallots), sliced diagonally
2 tablespoons chopped coriander
sesame oil to serve

1 Put the pork into a small pan, cover with boiling water, bring back to the boil and cook for 2 minutes; drain and reserve the liquid.

2 Soak the mushrooms in boiling water to cover for 20 minutes, then drain, adding the soaking liquid to the pork liquid. Discard the mushroom stems and slice the caps.

3 Soak the noodles in hot water to cover for 5 minutes, then drain and cut into 7.5cm (3 inch) lengths.

4 In a bowl, mix together the vinegar, sesame oil, soy sauce, sugar, chilli sauce and cornflour until smooth.

5 Put the chicken stock in a saucepan. Make the reserved liquid up to 625ml (1 pint/2½ cups) with water if necessary, add to the pan and bring to the boil. Add the pork, mushrooms, noodles and bean curd and simmer for 3 minutes.

6 Stir in the cornflour mixture and simmer, stirring, for 3 minutes until thickened.

7 Turn off the heat, then trickle in the egg from a fork, trailing it over the surface in a figure-of-eight movement; do not stir for about 30 seconds until the egg has set.

8 Gently stir in the spring onions (shallots) and coriander, with sesame oil to taste. *Serves 6.*

Mongolian Firepot

This soup is now popular throughout China with regional variations. Each person cooks his own food in a central pot of boiling stock and dips it into a sauce before eating. When most of the food has been cooked and the stock has a really strong flavour, noodles are added. The enriched stock is then consumed as a soup.

In China a special charcoal-burning firepot is used. As I do not possess such a thing, I use a large iron casserole dish over a spirit burner. Remember to provide everyone with a bowl, side plate, chopsticks and a wire strainer.

375g (12oz) Chinese cabbage
250g (8oz) spinach
750g (1½lb) lean lamb
90g (3oz) bean thread noodles
1.75 litres (3 pints/7½ cups)
  chicken stock
3 spring onions (green shallots),
  thinly sliced
2.5cm (1 inch) piece root (green)
  ginger, finely chopped
2 cloves garlic, finely chopped

SAUCE:
4 tablespoons tahini paste
2 tablespoons water
2 tablespoons soy sauce
2 tablespoons dry sherry
1-2 teaspoons chilli sauce
1 tablespoon sesame oil
1 tablespoon clear honey
1 tablespoon chopped coriander
  leaves

1 Cut the Chinese cabbage into 3.5cm (1½ inch) pieces. Remove the stalks from the spinach. Finely slice the lamb.
2 Soak the noodles in hot water for 5 minutes, then drain and cut into 7.5cm (3 inch) lengths. Arrange the cabbage, spinach, noodles and lamb on serving dishes.
3 To make the sauce, put the tahini in a small bowl and gradually blend in the water. Stir in the remaining ingredients. Transfer to individual serving bowls.
4 Put the stock in a large firepot or oven-to-table casserole. Add the spring onions (shallots), ginger and garlic and bring to the boil. Place on the spirit burner.
5 Each person cooks his own food using the small strainer, then dips it into the sauce. When all lamb and vegetables have been eaten, add the noodles to the stock, cook for a few minutes, then ladle the soup into bowls. *Serves 6.*

Zuppe Pavese

A speciality of Pavia, an old town in Italy, this is a meal in itself.
Use a good quality chicken or beef stock. If you prefer the egg white
to be cooked completely, first poach the eggs in the stock.

45g (1½oz) butter
4 thick slices bread
940ml (1½ pints/3 cups) stock
salt and pepper to taste

4 eggs
30g (1oz) Parmesan cheese,
* grated*
1 tablespoon chopped parsley

1 Melt the butter in a frying pan and fry the bread on
both sides until golden brown. Place in soup bowls and
keep warm.
2 Bring the stock to the boil in a pan and add seasoning.
Break an egg over each slice of bread and slowly pour on the
boiling stock; the egg will set as you pour.
3 Leave to stand for 1 minute, then sprinkle with Parmesan
and parsley to serve. *Serves 4.*

Portuguese Broad Bean Soup

500g (1lb) young shelled broad
* beans*
2 onions, chopped
2 cloves garlic, chopped
2 potatoes, chopped
salt and pepper to taste

1.25 litres (2 pints/5 cups)
* vegetable stock*
3 tablespoons olive oil
2-3 tablespoons chopped mint
2 teaspoons lemon juice
mint sprigs to garnish

1 Put the broad beans in a pan with the onions, garlic,
potatoes, seasoning and stock. Bring to the boil, cover and
simmer for 30 minutes. Allow to cool slightly.
2 Transfer to a blender or food processor, add the oil and work
to a purée. If the beans are large or if you use frozen ones, you
may need to sieve the soup to remove any tough skins.
3 Stir in the chopped mint and lemon juice. Reheat before
serving, garnished with mint. *Serves 6.*

Riojan Potato Soup

A rustic peasant soup from the Rioja area of Spain. Use a good quality chorizo sausage – strong, spicy and full of paprika, so that the flavour will permeate the soup and give it a pinky hue.

2 tablespoons olive oil
1 large onion, chopped
4 cloves garlic, chopped
750g (1½lb) potatoes, cut into
   chunks
940ml (1½ pints/3 cups)
   chicken stock

1 bay leaf
salt and pepper to taste
2 chorizo sausages, about 185g
   (6oz) total weight, sliced
2 tablespoons chopped parsley

1 Heat the oil in a pan, add the onion and fry until softened. Add the garlic and potato chunks and cook, turning, for 2 minutes until coated in oil.
2 Add the stock, bay leaf and seasoning. Bring to the boil, cover and simmer gently for 30 minutes until the potatoes are well cooked and beginning to break up.
3 Add the chorizo slices and parsley. Cook for a further 5 minutes to heat through. Remove the bay leaf before serving. *Serves 4.*

VARIATION: Replace the potatoes with 250g (8oz/1¼ cups) butter beans. Soak them overnight in cold water to cover, then drain and add to the soup with an additional 470ml (¾ pint/2 cups) stock. Cook the soup for 1½ hours, then add the chorizo and parsley and cook for 5 minutes.

Majorcan Chick Pea Soup

A rustic, peasant soup we always eat in a little restaurant in the back streets of Palma. It should be thick with vegetables and contain very little liquid.

250g (8oz/1¼ cups) chick peas,
*   soaked overnight and drained*
3 tablespoons olive oil
2 leeks, sliced
2 carrots, sliced
2 sticks celery, sliced
2 potatoes, chopped

397g (14oz) can chopped
*   tomatoes*
1 bay leaf
2 cloves garlic, chopped
salt and pepper to taste
½ small cabbage, shredded
125g (4oz) spinach, shredded

1 Put the chick peas in a saucepan, cover with cold water, bring to the boil and boil steadily for 10 minutes. Lower the heat, cover and simmer for 45 minutes.

2 Heat the oil in a saucepan, add the leeks, carrots and celery and cook gently for 15 minutes, stirring occasionally.

3 Drain the chick peas, reserving the liquid and make up to 1.25 litres (2 pints/5 cups) with water. Add the liquid to the vegetables with the chick peas, potatoes, tomatoes, bay leaf, garlic and seasoning. Cover and simmer gently for 40 minutes.

4 Add the cabbage and spinach and cook for a further 15 minutes. Discard the bay leaf.

5 Serve piping hot, with crusty bread. *Serves 6.*

Turkish Tomato Soup

1 tablespoon olive oil
2 cloves garlic, finely chopped
500g (1lb) tomatoes, skinned
  and chopped
315ml (10 fl oz/1¼ cups) tomato
  juice
salt and pepper to taste

1 tablespoon cornflour
TO FINISH:
155ml (5 fl oz/⅔ cup) natural
  yogurt
½ green pepper, seeded and
  sliced
2 pitta breads, toasted and diced

1 Heat the oil in a pan, add the garlic and fry for 1 minute.
Add the tomatoes and cook for 2-3 minutes. Add the tomato
juice with seasoning, and cook for 10 minutes.
2 Blend the cornflour with 155ml (5fl oz/⅔ cup) water, stir
into the soup and simmer, stirring, for 2 minutes.
3 Spoon the soup into warmed bowls, swirl some of the
yogurt into each portion and top with green pepper. Serve
the pitta bread separately. *Serves 4.*

Greek Bean Soup

250g (8oz/1¼ cups) haricot
  beans, soaked overnight
  and drained
1.25 litres (2 pints/5 cups)
  vegetable stock or water
2 cloves garlic, chopped
2 onions, chopped
3 sticks celery, chopped
3 carrots, chopped

397g (14oz) can chopped
  tomatoes
1 tablespoon tomato purée
  (paste)
3 tablespoons olive oil
2 tablespoons chopped parsley
1 bay leaf
salt and pepper to taste

1 Put the haricot beans in a saucepan with the stock or
water. Bring to the boil and boil steadily for 10 minutes.
Lower the heat, cover and simmer gently for 45 minutes.
2 Add the remaining ingredients and cook, covered, for a
further 1 hour until the beans are tender. *Serves 6.*

Lebanese Lentil Soup

Lentil soup is one of the most popular soups in the Middle East and there are many varieties. I particularly like this sustaining version, which was given to me by a Lebanese friend.

250g (8oz) brown lentils
2 carrots, chopped
1 potato, chopped
1.5 litres (2½ pints/6¼ cups)
  water
salt and pepper to taste
750g (1½lb) spinach or chard,
  stalks removed

4 tablespoons olive oil
1 onion, chopped
5 cloves garlic, chopped
1 teaspoon cornflour
juice of 1 lemon
2 tablespoons chopped coriander
  leaves

1 Put the lentils into a large saucepan with the carrots, potato, water and seasoning. Bring to the boil, cover and simmer gently for 45 minutes.

2 Chop the spinach or chard roughly and add to the saucepan, pressing it down well until it has wilted. Cover and simmer gently for 10 minutes.

3 Heat the oil in a frying pan, add the onions and fry gently for 2-3 minutes until pale golden. Add the garlic and cook for a further 2 minutes, then stir into the soup.

4 Blend the cornflour with the lemon juice and add to the soup with the coriander. Cook, stirring, for a further 2 minutes. Serve piping hot. *Serves 6-8.*

Dutch Meat Ball Soup

A Dutch favourite – a clear soup with miniature meat balls floating in it. Do use really lean meat for these. To enhance the flavour of the broth, replace half of the stock with a 425g (15oz) can consommé.

MEAT BALLS:
25g (1oz/½ cup) fresh
*   breadcrumbs*
125g (4oz) lean ground beef
125g (4oz) lean ground veal
1 egg
salt and pepper to taste
good pinch of nutmeg
⅛ teaspoon celery seeds
1 tablespoon chopped chervil

BROTH:
940ml (1½ pints/3¾ cups) clear
*   beef or chicken stock*
1 carrot
1 stick celery
1 leek
3 tablespoons dry sherry
3 tomatoes, skinned, seeded
*   and chopped*
1 tablespoon chopped chervil

1 Place all the ingredients for the meat balls in a food processor and blend until smooth, or mix thoroughly by hand.
2 Using dampened hands, form the meat into about 40 small balls, each the size of a cherry.
3 Bring the stock to the boil in a large pan. Add the meat balls and simmer gently for 8 minutes, removing the scum as it rises to the surface. Lift out the meat balls and set aside. Cool the stock and skim off all the fat.
4 Cut the carrot, celery and leek into julienne strips measuring 5cm x 3mm (2 x ⅛ inch).
5 Return the stock to the saucepan and bring to the boil. Add the vegetable julienne and simmer gently for 10 minutes. Add the sherry, tomatoes and chervil, with the meat balls. Heat through, then ladle into individual soup bowls to serve. *Serves 4-6.*

Goulash Soup

Magyar gulyás – or goulash – is Hungary's most famous dish. It is also served in the little mountain restaurants dotted all over the Austrian Tyrol. Richly flavoured with onion and paprika, this warming stew is a meal in itself.

2 tablespoons oil (approximately)
750g (1½lb) stewing beef, cut into 2.5cm (1 inch) cubes
2 onions, chopped
2 cloves garlic, chopped
1 tablespoon paprika
1 tablespoon flour
400g (14oz) can chopped tomatoes
940ml (1½ pints / 3¾ cups) beef stock

1 tablespoon tomato purée (paste)
1 teaspoon caraway seeds
salt to taste
2 large potatoes, chopped
1 red pepper, cored, seeded and chopped
TO SERVE:
155ml (5 fl oz / ⅔ cup) thick sour cream
1 tablespoon chopped parsley

1 Heat the oil in a pan, add the meat and fry briskly until evenly browned. Remove with a slotted spoon and set aside.
2 Add the onions to the pan, with a little more oil if necessary, and cook gently until softened. Add the garlic and paprika and fry very gently for 30 seconds, taking care to avoid burning the paprika. Remove from the heat and stir in the flour.
3 Add the tomatoes, stock, tomato purée (paste), caraway seeds and seasoning. Bring to the boil, stirring, then add the meat, cover and simmer very gently for 1½ hours until the meat is tender.
4 Add the potatoes and pepper and cook for a further 45 minutes.
5 Spoon into individual bowls, swirl a generous spoonful of sour cream into each portion and sprinkle with parsley to serve. *Serves 6-8.*

Swedish Yellow Pea Soup

A sustaining soup, served with slight variations throughout Scandinavia; this version of *gulartsoppe* was given to me by a Swedish friend. It is often accompanied by a glass of warm 'Punsch' a very sweet liqueur, and crisp rye biscuits with thin slices of cheese, such as Jarlsberg. I also like to serve *gulartsoppe* with coriander crackers (below).

500g (1lb/2½ cups) yellow split peas, soaked overnight and drained
1.75 litres (3 pints/7½ cups) water
2 onions, chopped
2 sticks celery, chopped
bouquet garni
500g (1lb) salt pork or bacon joint
salt and pepper to taste

1 Put the split peas into a large saucepan with the water and bring to the boil. Spoon off the scum that rises to the surface.
2 Add the onions, celery and bouquet garni. Cover and simmer gently for 45 minutes, then add the salt pork or bacon and cook for a further 1¼ hours until the peas are soft.
3 Take out the pork or bacon and cut the meat into pieces. Discard the bouquet garni.
4 Return the meat to the soup, add seasoning and a little more water to thin the soup if necessary. Serve with coriander crackers or chunks of rye bread. *Serves 8.*

CORIANDER CRACKERS: Put 60g (2 oz) wholemeal flour in a bowl with 1 teaspoon each ground coriander and caraway seeds, and a pinch of salt. Add 2 tablespoons water and mix to a firm dough. Knead until smooth, then chill for 10 minutes.

Shape the dough into 14 rounds, roll out very thinly into 7cm (3 inch) circles and bake in a preheated oven at 180C (350F/Gas 4) for 15 minutes, turning halfway through cooking. Cool on a wire rack.

Frankfurter Linsensuppe

3 tablespoons oil
2 leeks, sliced
2 carrots, chopped
2 sticks celery, chopped
250g (8oz/1¼ cups) green
  lentils, soaked in boiling
  water for 2 hours and drained

2 potatoes, chopped
1.75 litres (3 pints/7½ cups)
  stock or water
salt and pepper to taste
125g (4oz) smoked streaky
  bacon, chopped
350g (12oz) frankfurters, sliced

1 Heat the oil in a pan and gently fry the leeks, carrots, celery and garlic for about 20 minutes until softened.
2 Add the lentils, potatoes, stock or water, with seasoning and bring to the boil. Cover and simmer gently for 1 hour.
3 Fry the bacon in its own fat until crisp, then stir into the soup with the frankfurters. Add a little more water if the soup is too thick and heat through. *Serves 6.*

Choucroûtesuppe

1 tablespoon oil
1 onion, chopped
2 cloves garlic, chopped
125g (4oz) smoked streaky
  bacon, derinded and chopped
1 tablespoon flour
1.25 litres (2 pints/5 cups) stock

1 potato, finely chopped
500g (1lb) saurkraut, drained
227g (8oz) packet smoked pork
  sausage
250ml (8 fl oz/1 cup) thick sour
  cream
1 tablespoon chopped dill

1 Heat the oil in a pan and fry the onion, garlic and bacon until beginning to turn golden. Stir in the flour, then add the stock, potato and saurkraut. Bring to the boil and simmer for 15 minutes. Add the smoked sausage and simmer gently for a further 10 minutes.
2 Take out the sausage and cut into slices. Pour a ladleful of soup into the sour cream and mix well, then stir into the soup with the sausage and dill. Reheat very gently and serve with rye bread. *Serves 6-8.*

Borshch

There are many variations of this classic Russian soup, but they all include beetroot and thick sour cream or smetana. Borshch can be made as a thin soup to serve cold in the summer, or as a hearty hot vegetable soup.

This Ukranian borshch is full of vegetables and is a meal in itself. To make it even more substantial, chunks of beef are sometimes added. To prepare it this way, make a stock using 500g (1lb) shin of beef, an onion and bouquet garni and simmer for 2-3 hours. Use the beef stock for the soup; chop the meat and add it with the grated beetroot.

500g (1lb) beetroot, peeled
1 large onion, chopped
1 large potato, chopped
2 sticks celery, chopped
250g (8oz) cabbage, chopped
2 cloves garlic, chopped
1.25 litres (2 pints/5 cups) beef
   stock

1 bay leaf
salt and pepper to taste
1 tablespoon red wine vinegar
½ teaspoon sugar
155ml (5 fl oz/⅔ cup) thick sour
   cream or smetana
2 tablespoons chopped parsley

1 Set aside 125g (4oz) beetroot; chop the rest and put into a large saucepan with all the remaining vegetables, garlic, stock, bay leaf and seasoning.
2 Bring to the boil, cover and simmer gently for 45 minutes until the vegetables are tender.
3 Grate the remaining beetroot, add to the pan with the vinegar and sugar and cook for a further 15 minutes.
4 Spoon the borshch into individual serving bowls and swirl a large spoonful of sour cream or smetana into each portion. Sprinkle with parsley to serve. *Serves 6.*

Soupe de Poissons

The tiny fish used in Mediterranean fish soups are not available here, but a good result can be achieved using fish bones and trimmings, eg, sole, a few unshelled prawns and a little cheap fish. Toasted baguette, spread with rouille and topped with grated cheese, is the classic accompaniment.

2 tablespoons olive oil
1 onion, sliced
2 cloves garlic, chopped
175g (6oz) unshelled prawns
250g (8oz) conger eel, mullet or
  other cheap white fish
750g (1½lb) fish bones and
  trimmings, eg head of salmon
4 tomatoes, quartered
1 tablespoon tomato purée
  (paste)
bouquet garni
1.5 litres (2½ pints/6¼ cups)
  water

1 tablespoon white wine vinegar
salt and pepper to taste
¼ teaspoon powdered saffron
60g (2oz) vermicelli
ROUILLE:
½ red pepper, cored and seeded
2 red chillies, seeded
2 cloves garlic, chopped
60g (2oz/1 cup) fresh
  breadcrumbs
125 ml (4 fl oz / ½ cup) olive oil
TO SERVE:
1 baguette, sliced and toasted
grated gruyère cheese

1 Heat the oil in a large pan, add the onion, garlic, prawns, fish and bones and fry gently until lightly coloured. Add the tomatoes, purée (paste), bouquet garni, water, vinegar and seasoning. Bring to the boil, partially cover and simmer gently for 40 minutes.
2 Meanwhile make the rouille. Grill the red pepper, cut side down, until the skin blackens, then rinse off the black skin. Put into a blender or food processor with the chillies, garlic, breadcrumbs, 2 tablespoons fish liquor and seasoning. Blend until smooth, then gradually add the oil through the feeder tube, working until smooth. Transfer to a serving dish.
3 Discard any large pieces of bone, then strain the soup through a sieve, pressing through as much fish as possible.
4 Return to the rinsed-out saucepan and bring to the boil. Add the saffron and vermicelli and cook for 5 minutes.
5 Serve with the rouille, toast and cheese. *Serves 6.*

Mussel Chowder

This creamy chowder can also be made with clams which are prepared in the same way as mussels. Alternatively scallops can be used: you would need about 6 scallops which should be cooked for about 4 minutes, cut into pieces and added with the cream.

1.5kg (3lb) mussels in shells
625ml (1 pint/2½ cups) water
155ml (5fl oz/⅔ cup) white
  wine
1 tablespoon oil
1 clove garlic, crushed
125g (4oz) streaky bacon,
  rind removed, chopped

1 onion, chopped
1 tablespoon plain flour
2 potatoes, chopped
1 small leek, sliced
salt and pepper to taste
185ml (6 fl oz/¾ cup) single
  (light) cream
2 tablespoons chopped parsley

1 To clean the mussels, scrub them thoroughly, removing the beards and discarding any mussels that stay open when tapped.

2 Bring the water and wine to the boil in a large saucepan. Add the mussels, cover tightly and cook briskly for 3 minutes until they open; discard any that remain closed. Strain the liquid and reserve. Remove the mussels from their shells.

3 Heat the oil in the cleaned pan, add the garlic, bacon and onion, and cook gently for 5 minutes. Stir in the flour, then blend in the mussel liquid. Bring to the boil and cook, stirring, until thickened.

4 Add the potatoes, leek and seasoning. Bring to the boil, cover and simmer gently for 20 minutes.

5 Add the mussels, cream and parsley and reheat briefly. Serve immediately. *Serves 6.*

Lobster Bisque

One of the most delicious of all soups – to be reserved for very special occasions. Serve with croûtons (below).

1 small cooked lobster
30g (1oz) butter
1 tablespoon oil
1 onion, chopped
1 carrot, chopped
90g (3oz/½ cup) rice
250ml (8 fl oz/1 cup) dry white
    wine

1.75 litres (3 pints/7½ cups)
    fish stock
bouquet garni
90ml (3 fl oz/⅓ cup) double
    (thick) cream
60ml (2 fl oz/¼ cup) brandy
salt and cayenne pepper to taste

1 Lay the lobster on a chopping board with the hard shell uppermost and cut in half lengthwise. Open out the two halves and remove the black intestinal thread which runs down the tail, and the small sac in the head behind the eyes; these are the only parts to discard. The greenish liver should be retained.

2 Remove the tail meat, claw meat, liver and any coral and reserve.

3 Heat the butter and oil in a large saucepan, add the onion and carrot and cook until softened.

4 Add the lobster shells to the pan with the rice, wine, stock and bouquet garni. Cover and cook for 30 minutes.

5 Discard the lobster shells and bouquet garni. Transfer the contents of the saucepan to a blender or food processor, add the claw meat and liver and blend until smooth. Pass the soup through a sieve to obtain a really smooth texture. Return to the pan.

6 Mash the coral (if any) and stir into the soup with the cream, brandy and seasoning. Slice the reserved lobster tail meat, add to the soup and reheat gently. Ladle into individual serving bowls and serve immediately. *Serves 6.*

CROUTONS: Shallow fry 3mm (¼ inch) cubes of bread in hot oil until golden brown. Drain on absorbent kitchen paper.

Cullen Skink

Cullen is one of the little fishing villages on the Scottish Moray Firth where Finnan haddock is used to make this broth or 'skink'. If you cannot get Finnan haddock, use ordinary, naturally smoked haddock instead.

500g (1lb) Finnan haddock
625ml (1 pint/2½ cups) milk
30g (1oz) butter
1 onion, chopped
250g (8oz) potato, chopped

salt and pepper to taste
2 tablespoons chopped parsley
155ml (5fl oz/²⁄₃ cup) single
 (light) cream

1 Put the haddock in a shallow saucepan with the milk. Cover, bring almost to the boil and simmer very gently for 6-8 minutes.

2 Lift the fish out with a fish slice, transfer to a plate and allow to cool slightly. Strain the cooking liquid and make up to 625ml (1 pint/2½ cups) with milk if necessary.

3 Heat the butter in a pan, add the onion and fry until softened but not coloured. Add the potato and reserved liquid with seasoning. Bring to the boil, cover and simmer for 15 minutes until the potatoes are soft. Mash the potatoes in the liquor, using a potato masher.

4 Skin and flake the fish and add to the soup with the parsley and cream. Reheat gently and serve with herb and garlic croûtes. *Serves 4.*

HERB & GARLIC CROÛTES: Blend 60g (2oz) softened butter with 1-2 crushed garlic cloves and/or 1-2 tablespoons chopped parsley, marjoram or other herbs. Spread on to 8 slices of baguette and bake in a preheated oven at 220C (425F/Gas 7) for 10 minutes until crisp. Alternatively grill one side of the bread until toasted, turn and spread the non-toasted side with flavoured butter and grill until the edges begin to brown.

Fish Soup with Saffron

Saffron imparts a warm golden glow to this tasty soup. Served with garlic bread (below), it is a meal in itself. Leeks and fennel blend harmoniously with any white fish; I normally use a combination of monkfish, halibut and cod.

60g (2oz) butter
1 large leek, thinly sliced
1 small fennel bulb, thinly sliced
  lengthways
315ml (10 fl oz/1¼ cups) white
  wine
625ml (1 pint/2½ cups) fish
  stock
750g (1½lb) white fish, cut into
  2.5cm (1 inch) chunks

3 tomatoes, skinned and roughly
  chopped
½ teaspoon powdered saffron
2 tablespoons chopped parsley
1 tablespoon cornflour
2 tablespoons water
salt and pepper to taste
¼ teaspoon tabasco sauce
90ml (3 fl oz/⅓ cup) double
  (thick) cream

1 Melt the butter in a pan, add the leek and fennel, cover and cook very gently for about 15 minutes, stirring occasionally.

2 Add the wine and fish stock and simmer for 5 minutes. Add the fish chunks, tomatoes, saffron and parsley. Bring to a gentle simmer, cover and cook for 10 minutes.

3 Blend the cornflour with the water, add to the soup and cook for 1 minute until thickened. Season with salt, pepper and tabasco and stir in the cream. Serve immediately, with garlic bread if desired. *Serves 4-6.*

GARLIC BREAD: Mix 75g (3oz) softened butter with 2 crushed garlic cloves, 1-2 teaspoons chopped parsley if desired, and seasoning to taste. Make diagonal cuts through a French loaf at 2.5cm (1 inch) intervals, almost through to the base. Spread surfaces with flavoured butter. Wrap in foil and bake in a preheated oven at 200C (400F/Gas 6) for 15 minutes, loosening the foil for the last 5 minutes to crispen the top.

Caldeirada à Pescador

A popular soup all along the coast of Portugal, made from a mixture of white fish and shellfish – the choice and proportions of which can be varied according to personal taste and what is available.

It's a meal in itself and is ideal to serve outdoors in the summer, with white wine. Bibs and finger bowls are helpful as the shellfish need to be prised from their shells.

2 tablespoons olive oil
1 onion, chopped
1 red pepper, cored, seeded
  and chopped
2 cloves garlic, chopped
500g (1lb) tomatoes, skinned
  and roughly chopped
1 bouquet garni
625ml (1 pint/2½ cups) fish
  stock

315ml (10 fl oz/1¼ cups) dry
  white wine
salt and pepper to taste
750g (1½lb) mixed white fish
500g (1lb) mussels, scrubbed
250g (8oz) cooked prawns (in
  shell)
2 tablespoons chopped parsley

1 Heat the oil in a large pan, add the onion and pepper and cook gently for 10 minutes until softened.

2 Add the garlic, tomatoes, bouquet garni, stock, wine and seasoning. Bring to the boil, cover and cook for 10 minutes.

3 Cut the fish into 3.5cm (1½ inch) chunks, discarding the skin and bones. Add to the pan and cook gently for 3 minutes.

4 Add the mussels and cook for 5 minutes until their shells open; discard any that do not open. Add the prawns and heat through for 2 minutes. Discard the bouquet garni.

5 Turn into a large tureen, sprinkle with parsley and serve with chunks of bread and plenty of wine. *Serves 4.*

Avocado & Orange Soup

Citrus juice blends well with avocado and enhances its flavour in this recipe to give a subtle-tasting soup. Caviare-topped melba toasts are the ideal accompaniment.

1 large avocado
315ml (10 fl oz/1¼ cups) milk
315ml (10 fl oz/1¼ cups) natural yogurt
½ teaspoon grated onion
½ teaspoon Worcestershire sauce
salt and pepper to taste

155ml (5 fl oz/⅔ cup) thick sour cream
juice of 1 orange
TO SERVE:
melba toast (see below)
1 tablespoon lump fish roe
TO GARNISH:
few chives

1 Peel the avocado, halve, stone and cut into chunks. Put into a blender or food processor with all the remaining ingredients and blend to a smooth purée. Transfer to a bowl, cover and chill in the refrigerator for 30 minutes.

2 To serve, spoon the soup into individual bowls. Spoon a little caviare on to each melba toast and float on top of the soup. Garnish with chives to serve. *Serves 4-6.*

MELBA TOASTS: Preheat the oven to 160C (325F/Gas 3); preheat the grill, too. Toast the bread on both sides, cut off the crusts and slice in half horizontally to give wafer-thin slices. Cut diagonally into quarters and place on a baking sheet toasted side down. Bake in the oven for 10 minutes until curled.

Tomato & Basil Soup

Only make this soup when tomatoes are in season. They need to be sweet, juicy and really ripe to get a good flavour.

500g (1lb) tomatoes, skinned
3 tablespoons finely chopped
   basil
470ml (15 fl oz/1¾ cups) Greek
   strained yogurt

125ml (4 fl oz/½ cup) milk
salt and pepper to taste
basil sprigs to garnish

1 Chop the tomatoes finely and put into a bowl with the basil. Stir the yogurt with a fork until smooth, then add to the tomatoes with the milk and seasoning to taste. Mix well.
2 Cover and chill for about 1 hour before serving, garnished with basil. *Serves 4.*

Lettuce & Lovage Soup

A fragrant delicate soup that can be made with any type of lettuce; even the coarse outer leaves can be used. Also delicious served hot.

1 tablespoon oil
6 spring onions (green shallots),
   sliced
1 lettuce, shredded
1 lovage sprig, chopped
1 tablespoon flour

625ml (1 pint/2½ cups) boiling
   milk
salt and pepper to taste
90ml (3 fl oz/⅔ cup) double
   (thick) cream

1 Heat the oil in a pan and add the spring onions (shallots), lettuce and lovage. Cover and cook gently for 5 minutes. Stir in the flour, then gradually stir in the milk. Add seasoning, cover and simmer for 20 minutes. Allow to cool.
2 Purée the soup in a blender or food processor, then sieve if you prefer a really smooth texture. Stir in two thirds of the cream. Cover and chill for 1 hour.
3 To serve, pour into individual bowls and swirl in the remaining cream *Serves 4.*

Prawn & Almond Soup

The smoothness and subtle flavour of the almond soup blends unexpectedly well with the succulent prawns. If you have time, buy cooked prawns in their shells and peel them yourself – they will have a much better flavour.

125g (4oz) white bread, crusts
   removed
155ml (5 fl oz/²⁄₃ cup) milk
125g (4oz/1¼ cups) ground
   almonds
3 tablespoons lemon juice
3 tablespoons olive oil
1 small clove garlic, crushed

155ml (5 fl oz/²⁄₃ cup) single
   (light) cream
315ml (10 fl oz/1¼ cups) iced
   water
salt and pepper to taste
185g (6oz) shelled prawns
fennel sprigs to garnish

1   Break the bread into pieces and put into a bowl. Pour over the milk and leave to soak for 5 minutes.

2   Transfer the bread and milk to a blender or food processor and add the ground almonds, lemon juice, oil, garlic, cream, water, salt and pepper. Blend until smooth, then transfer to a bowl, cover and chill until required.

3   Spoon the soup into individual serving bowls, sprinkle each serving with prawns and garnish with fennel. *Serves 4.*

Gazpacho

The ever popular iced soup from Andalusia. Tomatoes ripened in Spain are plump, juicy and full of flavour – this is not always the case with the tomatoes we buy over here. If you can't find really good tomatoes, I suggest you replace half of the water with tomato juice to improve the flavour.

2 slices white bread, crusts
  removed
625ml (1 pint/2½ cups) cold
  water
750g (1½lb) ripe tomatoes,
  skinned and chopped
½ small onion, chopped
2 cloves garlic, crushed
½ cucumber, peeled and
  chopped
3 tablespoons olive oil
2 tablespoons white wine
  vinegar
salt and pepper to taste

TO SERVE:
2 slices bread
½ cucumber, diced
1 small onion, finely chopped
1 green pepper, cored, seeded
  and diced
1 red pepper, cored, seeded and
  diced

1 Break the bread into pieces and place in a bowl. Pour half of the water over the bread and leave to soak for 10 minutes.
2 Put the bread and soaking liquid into a blender or food processor with the tomatoes, onion, garlic, cucumber, oil, vinegar and seasoning to taste. Blend until smooth.
3 Pour into a soup tureen and stir in the remaining water. Chill in the refrigerator for about 1 hour.
4 Cut or break the bread into pieces and bake in a moderate oven for 15 minutes to crispen. Put the vegetable accompaniments into small serving dishes.
5 Pour the soup into individual bowls and serve with the crisp bread and accompanying vegetables *Serves 8.*

NOTE: If using tomato juice, as suggested above, add to the soup in step 3.

Morello Cherry Soup

*683g (1lb 6oz/4 cups) bottle
   Morello cherries, or 750g
   (1½lb) fresh ones
315ml (10 fl oz/1¼ cups) red
   wine
60g (2oz/¼ cup) caster sugar*

*1 large cooking apple, peeled,
   cored and chopped
3 cloves
½ teaspoon ground cinnamon
315ml (10 fl oz/1¼ cups) thick
   sour cream*

1 Drain the cherries and make the liquid up to 315ml
(10fl oz/1¼ cups) with water if necessary. Stone the cherries
and put into a pan with their liquid, the wine, sugar, apple
and spices. Bring to the boil, then cover and simmer gently
for 15 minutes. Discard the cloves.
2 Cool slightly, then purée in a blender or food processor.
Transfer to a bowl, cover and chill for 1 hour.
3 To serve, pour into individual soup bowls and swirl in the
sour cream. *Serves 6.*

Turkish Hazelnut Soup

*60g (2oz/½ cup) hazelnuts
1 clove garlic
2 tablespoons olive oil
315ml (10 fl oz/1¼ cups) milk
salt and pepper to taste*

*315ml (10 fl oz/1¼ cups) natural
   yogurt
¼ cucumber, peeled and
   chopped
1 tablespoon chopped dill
dill sprigs to garnish*

1 Put the nuts and garlic in a blender or food processor and
chop finely. Gradually add the oil, working to a smooth
purée, then add the milk and seasoning to taste. Blend
briefly to mix.
2 Put the yogurt in a bowl and stir until smooth, then
gradually stir in the hazelnut mixture with the cucumber
and chopped dill. Chill for about 1 hour.
3 To serve, pour into individual bowls and garnish with dill.
Serves 4.

Chicken Stock

One of the most useful of all stocks because its light flavour blends well with all types of soup.

1 chicken carcase	6 peppercorns
1 large carrot, sliced	salt to taste
2 sticks celery, sliced	1.75 litres (3 pints/7½ cups)
1 onion, quartered	water
bouquet garni	

1 Break up the carcase and put in a large pan with the giblets, vegetables, herbs, peppercorns and a little salt. Cover with the cold water and bring slowly to the boil.
2 Lower the heat, partially cover and simmer very gently for 1½-2 hours. Top up with boiling water if the level of the liquid falls below the top of the ingredients.
3 Strain the stock into a bowl and leave to cool. Refrigerate overnight so that the fat hardens into a solid layer on the top of the stock. Remove the fat layer. Use the stock as required.
Makes 1.25 litres (2½ pints/5 cups).

NOTE: If the stock is for immediate use, remove the grease by spooning it off the top, then floating a piece of kitchen paper on the surface to absorb the remaining fat; repeat several times if necessary.

Vegetable Stock

2 tablespoons oil	bouquet garni
2 onions, quartered	6 peppercorns
2 carrots, quartered	1 teaspoon salt
2 sticks celery, sliced	2.25 litres (4 pints/10 cups)
½ turnip, roughly chopped	water
few outer leaves from cabbage	

1 Heat the oil in a pan, add the vegetables and fry gently until pale golden, stirring occasionally.

2 Add the bouquet garni, peppercorns and water and bring to the boil. Partially cover the pan and simmer gently for about 3 hours. Strain the stock into a bowl and leave to cool. Refrigerate and remove any fat before using. Use as required. *Makes 1.75 litres (3 pints/ 7¹/₂ cups).*

NOTE: When boiling vegetables, strain the liquid and keep in the refrigerator. Use in place of the above stock or instead of the water.

Fish Stock

A well-flavoured fish stock makes all the difference to a fish soup. Ask your fishmonger for fish bones and trimmings and he will usually be happy to give you some. Sole bones are perfect, as they are gelatinous and full of flavour. You will often be able to buy a head of salmon or conger eel, but remove the gills first. Although cod heads are usually removed at sea nowadays, you may be able to get cod ears instead. Shellfish shells and a few whole prawns enhance the flavour too.

1kg (2lb) sole bones and fish	*6 peppercorns*
trimmings	*1 teaspoon salt*
bunch of parsley	*125ml (4 fl oz/ ¹/₂ cup) white wine*
1 bay leaf	*1.75 litres (3 pints/ 7¹/₂ cups)*
1 onion, quartered	*water*

1 Put all the ingredients in a large pan, making sure they are well covered with water. Bring to the boil, partially cover and simmer gently for about 40 minutes.
2 Strain into a bowl, pressing through as much liquid as possible. Use as required. *Makes 1.25 litres (2¹/₂ pints/5 cups).*

Index